Frozen Sunsets

Soulshine & Stardust

Chelsey Wellsted

Made with ❤ on the BookLeaf Publishing Platform
www.bookleafpub.in
www.bookleafpub.com

Dedication

To my children who always have stars sparkling in their eyes, love in their hearts, and souls full of kindness; and to my husband who always makes it possible for me to reach for my dreams and goals.

Preface

Writing and speaking through poems or lyrics has always been part of me as long as I remember. I have always searched for the beauty of this world in everyday moments, even those that challenge and teach us how to move forward by looking deep within ourselves to find the strength to do so. Share your heart with the world and never miss a chance to gaze upon the stars, see the sunset, listen to the stillness of a quiet snowfall, and have meaningful conversations with those you love.

Acknowledgements

Thank you to all the generations before me whose choices brought me into this life, and to all those who read this when my soul has moved on. Never forget the power of the words you choose to use- they are the most important freedom we have.

My hope is that at the end of it all I have made a difference, I have led with love and care, helped others and brought kindness to those who need it the most. And, above this all, I stay true to myself and others in my journey.

AN AUTUMN DESCENT

With sure signs another fall is preparing it's beautiful entrance
Clues such as crunching acorns
A chilling north wind against our face
Pine cones to help us start bonfires
The still warmth glitters from the sun upon the water
We wait

We wait for the change
As we wait for the snow to melt away in the spring
The autumn warmth is upon us like an old friend with an enduring hug

The wind carries along with it distant sounds from lands far away
Beyond our reach, a memory
We know the familiar sounds fluting across the water
As reeds dance in the wind
Birds plan their travel south as they chirp their good byes and wish us well

By the end of this early autumn day
The wind works to clear the sky with all its might
To share on the horizon one more time

The opportunity to experience the magical coloration of the sky
Mirroring the water blending together
The blues, pinks, and oranges
It slowing descents away and hands off to the night sky

Tiny lights begin to twinkle
As if someone is turning them on with a serene swipe
Thousands upon thousands of stars appear in layers
Revealing themselves and greeting us
As they take their moment within the night
The moon makes her grand entrance to lead us home
Until we meet again under the autumn sky

A MILLION SUNS

Yesterday I woke up to a million suns instead of one
And even though the sky was so dark
Light still found its way through
Starshine fell across the early morning

No one else was awake
Silence beamed through the air and I wondered
How can I capture this beautiful morning
No pictures could satisfy the view

I sat against the window and watched the twinkle of the constellations
The mysterious beauty it gave
The subtle silhouette to the evergreens and pines reaching
The edge of the globe surrounding me

With a blanket draped around me, I stepped through the door
Into the magic of a million suns sparkling down to earth
Twirling around to see the familiar twinkle
Endless depths against the deep blank canvas

Each star has been placed so perfectly chaotic

Exactly where they were meant to be
Stardust filled my eyes as tears do
When someone touches your soul and brings your heart

To the edge of an endless night
The brilliance we live with everyday
If only each day we would start it this way
So today I woke again to a million suns instead of one

THE STILLNESS OF MORNING

I love the stillness of the early morning
The hours before the light
When you feel the only one awake is you
Enjoying the last moments of the night

Even before the sun
The light shows us the world
Beyond the shadows
That stretch to cover us in darkness

But darkness does not last forever

ALONG THE SHORE

I stood along the shore
Urged into the water
Strong wind blowing the waves
Crashing into the rocks
And something else
Some unknown breathe I so needed
A breathe saying this is being in the moment
Your feet in the cool water
The wind in your hair
And nothing else but this
I closed my eyes
Felt it completely to my soul
I didn't want to leave

THE POEMS OF OUR SOULS

We move with loud souls and quiet mouths
Through the nights of time
In a brilliant life of sorrows and joys
We mostly do this alone in places of solitude
Moments of strength spiraling through
The stories of our lives
Verses in the poems of our souls
Reaching back to the lines
They speak out loud
You heard it said
By some unknown voice
Thousands of years before

WITHOUT EACH OTHER

It's the moments of life that give us our biggest challenges
Our most concerning hesitations we tend to turn away from
Our avoidance of the failure
We don't want to feel
This is the cost of success
We sacrifice to protect ourselves
We hold our own away from the world
No one can see who we are trying to be
We shy away from the chance
We are lonely
We are lost
We need each other
This is the only way through to push up through all the stops along the way
To pull each other from the sinking sand
Up to the shore
We connect to the elements of this life
Finding the energy to continue on
Because another soul cared enough to take our hands

TATTOOS OF FREEDOM

He walks with his head high
Although it seems to be a tireless struggle
His mind and body have been through more pain
Than anyone should ever bear

Most nights he sleep mere hours
On edge, on defense, on a stand-to
Ready to battle the ghosts
Waiting for him in his dreams

He wakes and drags through the days
The pain constant through his body
Reminding him of the battles
Continuing on through his memories

They have become part of his being
The bullet holes, the shrapnel
Embedded in his bones
A smaller price than others

The tattoos to remind him
Remind him of the cost
The lives and pain of others
We exchange for our freedoms

All for our freedom
The pain we don’t see
The loss we don’t feel
The hate we will never know
The lives they could have lived
The duty they are chained to
The love they sacrificed

For us, our freedom
Our flag, our country
The ideals, the opportunities
Our lives because

The soldiers never stop
Will not stop
The forever battle
We call freedom

A VETERAN'S LOVE

Every button and string perfectly done
As he remembers the lives laid down for everyone
Unsure of his continued existence
Finding it hard to believe
Wondering why he lives
Always asking why not me

He sees all their faces
Embedded in thought every time
He hears another soldier has been lost
To war, anger, or self defeat
He struggles to continue
His proud stance on two feet

But he does not give up on his protection
Of this country and her flag
He holds in the highest affection
It breaks his heart to see her trampled and burned,
Spit on and ripped
With absolutely no concern

About the lives he remembers
That protected her so
The ones she now protects

Six feet below

His soldier soul will always remain
As he continues his proud stance daily in pain
The veteran
With his head held high
Raises his love for this country,
The American Flag to the sky

FALL FALL FALL

I leave my heart wide open
As I spin round round round
And the rain falls down down down
And I fall fall fall
In love with you

From the start
In the dark
Under the stars
In your arms
In my dream
Fall awake
From sleep
It's not real
Only me
Let it be

We are only friends
But could have been
Something more
Bottom of the floor
Trying to fly
With broken wings
Can't talk can't sing

Only catching each other looking
No words are said
It's all in our heads
We can't explain
The pouring rain

As drops fall fall fall
And love comes crashing down down down
We spin round round round
Stuck in a place I can't erase
From my heart
The night we danced in the rain
Was that our start or our end
Will we ever find our love again

SHIMMER

Now that I have found you
I don't want to let you go
All I want to do is see you
But I am not sure you even know

I don't want to scare you
I will keep my distance from here
Maybe one day one time it is okay
To be close and near

I am not sure why this is happening
I can't think of anything else
What I am putting myself through
It's not really any help
I'm swirling in a spiral in a place I don't know
I think my soul is finally full

It's like I finally see that the one
I have been looking for is finally near
I don't want to take the chance
I have too much to lose
When I am in your presence
I am unbalanced in my stance

Words stall
I am frozen at the chance to say
The words are crashing smashing together
They make no sense because no matter
The reason we have been brought together is maybe
The chance of the daily weather

I am falling apart on the inside
All I can do is smile
I don't want to have the truth coming out for a while
I am not even sure that you are right for me
It's like a meet cute in a romantic comedy
There is just something about you

I can't bring my thoughts to a stop
I wish they would stop
There is so much at risk for even the thought
I miss the opportunity to see what we could become over time slowly
I just don't want to be in passing
I would rather check out what could be everlasting

In a world that moves too fast
In moments that can feel like a glass falling
To the ground and catching it
Before it shatters all around
Beautifully breaking across the floor

But broken glass can shimmer even more brightly than before

And missing one shard can cause enough pain
Bring me down from the soul pain
Because it's like I knew you before
I even opened the door
Now I am drawn in
I can't even begin to know this disaster

The mess this could cause
I am giving myself pause
To slow down and cherish these moments that are precious to me
Before these moments become distant memories

If meeting you as if on queue
An unbelievably new feeling at once
It's as if I have known you forever in my soul
I am not even sure you know

SHADOWS AND SOULS

Pouring over the disdain
Living under my own pain
Where my heart lives
Contemplating

I can't stop
Knowing your existence
It's unbearable
I am in resistance

Of a love I don't know
A love on the down low
The unbearable toll
Waiting for you the love of my soul

Our shadows dance together at night
Dreams of each other colliding
Passing by one another in morning light
There no way of this feeling subsiding

I stumble over my words when I see you
I notice you do too
Or am I imagining a false connection
Another let down, a failure of my own loves complexion

I don't know the way out of this
There really is not a way to grant my soul's wish
Maybe one day we will find our way
Even if we are years away being able to stay

In each other's presence
Beyond moments passing
Shadows and souls
Are the best for dreams untold

SHARDS OF ICE

I didn't think you could break my heart
So much I couldn't breath
Broken pieces torn apart
Words aren't what I need

How could you throw away our love
I don't understand where we fell apart
Downward spiraling
Like shards of ice falling from the sky

Crashing down, broken pieces all around
Broken pieces that melt
And never can be put back together the same way
Nothing is the same anymore

There are no new starts for us
Just memories that were pretend
Til we finally meet our end
Not even friends after this pain

It's exhausting from the chances that made no sense
No more hope is left
Just empty souls
That were never meant to be together

Instead we would have been better
To pass by and fill years with less tears
Tears that are now empty
And instead stay inside

Drowning out the cries and pain
Quietly staying and refrained
From letting go and moving on
Where we should go but can't

Because we live in this cycle of brokenness and despair
Where we are only losing ourselves
Love unshared, stumbling through the days
Acting like we are both okay

We are broken in the inside
The pain is starting to show through
We become see through
We can't hide the pain anymore

SOULS APART, WORLDS TOGETHER

Months go by
You seem to have disappeared
But then you visit my dreams like a ghost
I rarely know you but still the same
In my dreams it seems that we know each other closely by name

My soul feels connected to you and when we see each other there is nothing we can do
Because we belong to others
In reality
But we must belong to each other when we dream

I can't explain to myself how and why
Those nights I dream of you close by
As if we were together long ago
Connected to each other's souls

And maybe in dreams this is what is true
When we can be ourselves, we do
What our hearts truly yearn
Centuries spent apart just to learn

How truly our souls are connected
Even if life gets in the way
Dreams have a way of finding
A place for us to be together

And these dreams pull us closer
And in life too
We know each other
But can't be like we want to

And maybe we wait or maybe we leap
Either we fall or land on our feet
Pulling each other up from the ashes of the past
And finding another way to be together at last

ANOTHER TIME

I think I love you in a way
I love no one else
It's the feeling the songs all sound like
A desired state of experience
Out of reach and unknown
My heart changes what I see you
Or hear your voice

You are the heaviest weight
That pulls on my heart and whatever I do
Everything I try
I can't stop thinking that our souls are connected

Somehow
Maybe in another time
Another place
Another life

It's the strangest thing because it's an anticipation
An amazing feeling to know you made it one more day
in this life
That you continue to be

And one day our souls will

Connect somewhere in
An unforgettable moment
Permanently and uninterrupted

WHEN POCKETS DANCE

How I do adore pockets, they are of many use
A place to put your hands, trinkets, money or when something falls loose
Dresses with pockets, they are my favorite, hidden slightly at the seams
Of dancing flowing fabric, they are hard to believe when actually seen

As for pockets in jeans, we seem to abandon
Pens, money, notes, jewelry, gum, so many things that need to be undone
If not emptied they cause a great mess, sticky and gluey, black and blue
Lost things all because of "You Pockets You!"

Now the responsibility is hard to delegate
It's the owner of the pockets we have to investigate
Because we need to hinge the relationship
Of the garment journey to this predicament

Who wore it, and where did they go
Why did they forget to unpocket their pockets
Before they were so easy to throw
Them right into the basket

And who carried the basket to the room where they wash
Why didn't they check each garment before they tossed
Them into the washer when the pen cover came off and the gum got wet
Oh why oh why but I am willing to bet

When we switched to the dryer and added some heat
We didn't even notice the ink filled leak
And those pockets we should have unpocketed have a new look
Along with some friends they danced with as the washer shook

So by the time we are aware
We likely need more than a new pair
And nobody and anybody knows
But one thing I know is certain

I do adore pockets, I really do
But be careful of others who have pockets too!

TWOS DAY

Today is a day of twos
But it's also the day of Tues
Zero Two Zero Two Two Zero Two Two
So when the clock shows Two two two
It will be Two Twenty Two on the Tuesday of Two
Twenty Two in the year of Two Thousand Twenty Two
That's a lot of two, to do anything you want to do on the day of double twos, month of two, the year of twos, decade of twos and the millennium of twos too!

So on this Tuesday or Twos Day of Twos what are you to do with all the twos?

You could toot toot toot toot too
You could to da to da to da to
You could to to to to to to to
In French you may say "Tu vais Toi" which is another Tu for you to consider too!

Or you can just take two, I think that is what I will do too!

HIDDEN HAVEN

There is a grove of trees
Along the river that hides an old road
Hidden in the bluffs only those
Who have lived there long enough know

There is one path that leads the way
That winds through the woods
Past a pasture of gold that glitters
With the touch of the sun

And shows them the way home
Once there you find magic
A place of peace so calm
Where time is lost and fortune is found

Take the last road in town
Follow down along the way
Down two hills
And past the deer forest

Beyond the field of dreams
Find the trees you can climb to touch the sky
There is a magical garden
Where the cottage sits two stories high

Through no man’s land
And much further down
The black road
To the hidden path

The last house before the path
Guards the secrets of this world

DISCONNECT

I have been trying to get away from the world
Just for a while
Looking for a space
To hide away my smile

I am struggling to disconnect because I am discontent
With what I read and see
I am starting to wonder
What is wrong with me

My objection is pretty simple
And also complicated to explain
Nobody wants to feel
Or express their true pain

We hide behind the pictures
We want others to see
We write as we drown
In a sea of me and me and me

Excuse my exit of this madness
It's time has run its course
All we do is connect
To disconnect

A vision of appeal
A vision that is not real
To be me but not the me
I want the world to see

LOSE OURSELVES

How easy it is to forget who I am
The way we lose ourselves to prioritize others
Emptying our hearts
Through tears

Why is it that we allow
Ourselves to become so pulled in
That somehow we lose parts of ourselves
Along the way

And yet we find
New parts of this life
That replace what we have lost
Filling our hearts again

Or is it
That we were always lost

From the very beginning
And each moment we have
Each choice we have
Changes who we are

Time brings us closer

To the infinity of our souls
Each tear lost
Is a measure of our hearts

Each hand we hold
Each hug we give
Every smile we share
Brings us closer

Closer to each other
Hearts that become intertwined
Can never be pulled apart
Not completely

We come back
To these moments
Of our dreams
Not coincidentally

Because we know
We are more
Or could have been more
For each other

TO JUST BE

We take advantage of this world
We are no longer humbled by our own existence
Instead selfish
Undeserving

We forget to appreciate the mornings that give us light
and the nights that give us rest
We value the artificial more than the natural
The instant gratification
Instead of the earned results

We are not able to separate from the work
Because if we do
It is perceived as not caring
Not showing up

I am starting to think why do we bring ourselves
Through so much misery, through falseness
We cannot be accepted fully
For who we want to be

I think it is time to change how the world is
Change what it is to become
To bring our souls forward

To bring light, to bring rest

To just be without needing to be what others want to see

A WORLD I DON'T BELONG

I live in a world I don't belong
Because this world has lost most of it's love
Anger fills the hearts of others, towards others
Who have not done anything wrong

We try to walk on rainbows but fall right through
Imagining places better than here
Where birds can fly
But we can't seem to find the way

Lost
Displaced
Ignored
Alone

Maybe one day we can heal
Hearts can see beyond our vision
We can build a world
Where our souls can be free

WE BELONG TO THE STARS

Stars are known to be born in pairs
Separated at creation
Like our souls
Who know we need our true connection

And what if each soul had a star it belonged to
When a star is born
A soul is also born
Everlasting, stars and souls in passing

As our souls travel through time
Across worlds
Searching for our pair
Finding their way home

In each life
We leave a trail
Of stardust behind
For our soulmates to find

Our stars fade as our souls fade
Slowly in solitude
Until our souls finally connect again

And we go back to where the souls began

We belong to the stars, our eternal resting place
As we belong to each other, together at last
Stuck in the black holes
Now shining bright with our souls

www.ingramcontent.com/pod-product-compliance
Lightning Source LLC
LaVergne TN
LVHW020406290726
844417LV00033B/326

* 9 7 8 9 3 6 9 5 4 7 1 0 4 *